WOODENISMS

The Wisdom and Sayings of Coach John Wooden

Neville L. Johnson

Cool Titles
439 N. Canon Dr., Suite 200, Beverly Hills, CA 90210
www.cooltitles.com

The Library of Congress Cataloging-in-Publication Data Applied For

Neville L. Johnson—
Woodenisms: The Wisdom and Sayings of Coach John Wooden

p.   cm
ISBN 978-1-935270-43-0
1. SPO061010 SPORTS & RECREATION / Coaching / Basketball
2. BUS046000 BUSINESS & ECONOMICS / Motivational
3. SPO041000 SPORTS & RECREATION / Sports Psychology

I. Title   2016

Printed in the United States of America

1 3 5 7 9 10 8 6 4 2

Book editing and design by Lisa Wysocky, White Horse Enterprises, Inc.

ALL QUOTES FROM COACH WOODEN

HAVE BEEN PRINTED IN ORIGINAL FORM.

For interviews or special discounts for bulk purchases, please contact cindy@cooltitles.com

Also by Neville L. Johnson

The John Wooden Pyramid of Success

What Took You So Long

Dedication

To all teachers, coaches, and students.

Acknowledgements

To Coach Wooden—without whom this book would not exist—for his wisdom. To the many journalists and writers who captured Coach's words for posterity.

Table of Contents

Introduction

JOHN WOODEN MATTERS BECAUSE OF HIS VALUES, experience, insights, and example. This is a book of his sayings, "Woodenisms," a phrase coined by his grandson-in-law, Craig Impelman, who compiled some of them more than twenty years ago. I was able to add to the list during my research for *The John Wooden Pyramid of Success,* the authorized biography of Coach Wooden that I wrote. Of all I have ever done I am most proud of writing that book, in part because it was also the hardest endeavor I've ever taken on. There is so much to learn about—and then say about—this legendary, beloved sports figure. Moreover, focusing on Wooden and his wisdom changed my life for the better in all respects.

Coach lived a balanced life where family came first, but work obviously got done and there was time for friends and relaxation. John Wooden passed away June 4, 2010, but his legacy lives on in the many people he inspired, and in his ideas that are so helpful to us all. Love, integrity, and class are three words that Wooden personified.

As a basketball coach, Wooden's records are not just unequaled; they are unapproachable and legendary. His UCLA teams won the national championship ten times in a twelve year period—seven years in row, with four undefeated seasons. Wooden is widely considered by both sports journalists and the public to be the greatest coach of all time in any sport, but he was more proud of being a husband, father, and teacher. Coach Wooden is rightly one of the most respected persons ever. Awards are named after him, and many bestselling books have now been written about and with him.

Wooden exemplified and lived the ideals in the sayings in this book. He was the real deal—and truly humble, kind, personable, charming and witty. He loved people, life, and was a joy to be around. It is how he lived and what he had to say where he has made his greatest impact.

More than anything else, Wooden was a philosopher. His Pyramid of Success, the no-nonsense, brilliant, non-sectarian strategy for living that he created is a masterpiece. It is his magnificent gift to humankind.

The following sayings, these profound teachings of Coach Wooden, will inspire, motivate, and prepare you for any challenge you face. They will also help you enjoy the good times. These perfect nuggets of wisdom have done that for me. Hardship comes in many forms: economic, romantic, spiritual, emotional, physical. That's life. It's how we cope with the larger issues that face us that matters.

Woodenisms provide good common sense, and I hope you distribute them freely and widely at home, work, and play. They will assist you in being a leader and a team player. Woodenisms will also give you strength to carry on in whatever you do. Their pedigree, of course, is gold standard. Obviously they work, as Coach has proven.

Many of these Woodenisms have been distributed for years with great usefulness and value to student-athletes, business persons, and attendees at seminars. They have also been used in magazines and newspapers; and in presentations by Coach Wooden and other speakers. Now they are collected here, yours to cherish and enjoy as you strive for success.

Neville Johnson
July 2016

Individual Improvement

When you are through learning,
you are through.

Never lose faith or patience.

It's not what you think you are,
but what you think.

If you're too busy making a living,
you're not going to make much of a life.

I will get ready
and then perhaps my chance will come.

Forget favors given,
remember those received.

I am what I am.
I don't worry what others think of me.

Consideration for others
brings many things.

Don't beat yourself.
It will be the worst kind of defeat
you will ever suffer.

Everything revolves around faith,
family and friends.

Acquire peace of mind by
becoming the best that
you are capable of being.

If you keep too busy
learning the tricks of the trade,
you may never learn the trade.

People are usually as happy
as they make up their mind to be.

It is what you learn after you know it all
that counts.

It's up to you.

You have nothing to fear
if you have prepared
to the best of your ability.

The way you think will be
the way that you will play.

Don't let making a living
prevent you from making a life.

It is important to recognize that you are
totally in control of your success—
not your opponent, the judge, critic,
media, or anyone else.

"Love" is the most important word
in the English language,
followed by "balance."

Make friendship an art.

Disagree without being disagreeable.

Slow and steady gets you ready.

Earn the right to be proud and confident.

Never expect favors, alibi or make excuses.

Mistakes occur when your thinking
is tainted by excessive emotion.

True happiness comes from the things
that cannot be taken away from you.

Never say never.

Learn as if you were to live forever,
live as if you were to die tomorrow.

If your complaints are constant,
serious and genuine about your calling,
then leave when practical.

Self-control keeps you in the present.

A winner never quits;
a quitter never wins.

There is no progress without change,
though change is not necessarily progress.

Be a gentleman at all times.

"I do it because he does it,"
is not a good reason.

If you are going nowhere,
you'll get there.

Passion is momentary;
love is enduring.

Have courage and do not worry.

All material things can be taken away.

Without faith and courage you are lost.

No matter how fine a person is at anything,
he can always improve.

Ability may get you to the top,
but it takes character to keep you there.

It is not what you do,
but how well you execute it—
if it is based on sound valid principles.

Serenity is ever with those
who are considerate of
and courteous to others.

No one ever reaches
maximum potential.

You cannot live a perfect day
without doing something
for someone who will never
be able to repay you.

The great secret of life is to
cultivate the ability to appreciate
the things you have,
not compare them.

Ability is a poor man's wealth.

Discipline yourself
and others won't have to.

Do not mistake activity
for achievement.

If you do not have time to do it right,
when will you have time to do it over?

You may make mistakes,
but you are not a failure until
you start blaming someone else.

If you are afraid of criticism,
you will die doing nothing.

The smallest good deed
is better than the
greatest intention.

Don't let yesterday
take up too much of today.

Time spent getting even would be
better spent getting ahead.

There is nothing in this world
stronger than gentleness.

You can do more good
by being good than in any other way.

When success turns your head,
you face failure.

Love is the medicine that can cure
all the ills of the world.

35

There is no pillow as soft
as a clear conscience.

Revenge is the weak pleasure
of a little and narrow mind.

A good memory
is one that can remember
the day's blessings and
forget the day's troubles.

The true athlete should have character,
not be a character.

The future may be when you wish
you had done what you are not doing now.

The greatest conquest of man
is the conquering of himself.

Talent is God given, be humble;
fame is man given, be thankful;
conceit is self-given, be careful.

More often than we ever suspect,
the lives of others we affect.

Your reputation is what others think you are,
your character is what you really are.

It is steady progress that we want
and it will come with industry and patience.

Mental, moral, and physical individual
and team balance are essential.

45

A wonderful mystical law of nature
that the three things we crave most in life—
happiness, freedom and peace of mind—
are always attained by giving them
to someone else.

46

Keep courtesy and consideration of others
foremost in your mind.

Pray for guidance and strength
to do your best, and then have faith.

Although it may not be possible
to determine what happens to you,
you should control how you
react and respond.

Try to have fun without being funny.

Never try for a laugh at another's expense.
Try to laugh with others, never at them.

You meet the same people on the way up
as you meet on the way down.

The Golden Rule may well be
the basic concept of every religion.

Do unto others, as you would
have them do unto you.
(The Golden Rule).

The harvest of old age
is the recollection and abundance
of blessings previously secured.

Life is not all good, nor is it all bad.
What mortal man can separate
the many gray areas
into good
and bad?

Repetition is
the last law of learning.

Teamwork

Happiness begins
where selfishness ends.

Politeness is a small price to pay
for the goodwill and affection of others.

The best way to improve the team
is to improve yourself.

The main ingredient of stardom
is the rest of the team.

Life is a united effort of many.

Be a team player always.

Your team will be judged
by your appearance
and your conduct.
May you command
the respect of all
in both.

59

Good manners should
control your actions at all times.

Never be selfish, jealous,
envious, or egotistical.

Teams win or lose games,
not individuals or coaches.

It takes a lot of little things
to make one big thing.

What is right is more important
than who is right.

Never criticize, nag, or razz
a teammate.

Quickness, not size,
is the most important aspect
of athletics.

It's not important who starts the game,
but who finishes it.

64

Sports do not build character;
they reveal it.

It's impossible to do something
for someone else
without doing something
for yourself
at the same time.

Courtesy and politeness
are a small price to pay
for the good will and affection
of others.

It is amazing how much can be accomplished
if no one cares who gets the credit.

Winning takes talent, to repeat takes character.

The athlete who says something
cannot be done
should never interrupt
the one who is doing it.

Consider the rights of others
before your own feelings,
and the feelings of others
before your own rights.

69

There is so much good in the worst of us,
and so much bad in the best of us,
there can hardly be room for any of us
to talk about the rest of us.

70

We all want to do well
and achieve individual praise.
That is fine if you put it to use
for the good of the team, be it sports,
business, family, or community.

Team spirit begins in the home,
where it must, and then extends
out to all other areas throughout the world.

Overcoming Adversity

We get stronger morally
and spiritually
through adversity.
It's only going to
make us stronger.

Adversity is the state in which man
most easily becomes acquainted with himself,
being especially free of admirers then.

Success is giving 100 percent of your effort, body, mind, and soul to the struggle.

Things turn out best for those
who make the best of the way things turn out.

Wouldn't it be a wonderful world
if everyone magnified their blessings
as much as their sorrows?

Don't give up on your dreams
or your dreams will give up on you.

Failure is not fatal,
but failure to change may be.

In the final analysis, perhaps
the most important thing we need
in all walks of life is more mutual trust,
faith, and understanding of the
problems of others.

Never make excuses.
Your friends won't need them
and your foes won't believe them.

Don't let what you cannot do
interfere with what you can do.

Bad times can make you bitter or better

Don't measure yourself
by what you have accomplished,
but by what you should have accomplished
with your ability.

You have success within.
It is up to you to bring it out.

Complaining, whining, making excuses
just keeps you out of the present.

83

It's the little details that are vital.
Little things make big things happen.

A man makes mistakes,
but he isn't a failure
until he starts blaming
someone else.

If you lose self-control
everything will fall.

You have conquered fear
when you have initiative.

You cannot function physically or mentally or in any other way unless your emotions are under control.

Never fear failure.
It is something to learn from.

Failure rests with those who stay
on some success made yesterday.

To do better in the future
you have to work on
the "right now."

Dwelling in the past
prevents doing something
in the present.

Although it would be great if we never had to face adversity, the fact is that it only makes us stronger—be it physically, mentally, morally or spiritually.

[O]ne should never become
too dependent upon others
for the solution of personal problems.
Talking them over, however,
to a friendly ear can be of help.
I have found prayer to be the most
helpful when I am troubled,
and believe that all prayers are heard
and answered, even though
the answer is no.

91

Success is not perfection,
which you can never obtain.
Nevertheless, it is the goal.

Leadership

If you're a great teacher
and you don't have any knowledge,
what are you going to teach?

Respect is something that has to come
from how you treat the players,
the game itself, and your preparation.
It cannot be demanded from the players.

The two most important elements
in coaching are the knowledge that's
necessary and the rapport, the company
you have with those that you're trying to teach.

I'd rather have talent than experience.

Your team must be receptive,
and it is up to you to make them receptive.

97

There are no secrets.

An unbeatable five consists of
industriousness, enthusiasm,
condition (mental, moral, and physical),
sound fundamentals, and proper team spirit.

It's what you do during the week.
There's very little you can do during the game.

Study and learn all you can
from all those with whom you come in contact,
and that is not only other coaches,
but all others.

The ideal level of motivation
is nothing other than consistent
preparation and execution that starts
the first day of practice and is maintained
at a constant level throughout the season.

It is up to you to have
the proper teaching techniques
to be able to get it across.

Those who have never suffered adversity,
never experience the true meaning of success.

You get ideas across better
through listening and the pat-on-the-back method
than you do with a kick in the pants.

Sometimes winning hides problems,
but sometimes it creates some of its own.

Whenever you bring together
a group of intelligent, highly motivated
individuals, you are going to have conflicts.

We coaches sometimes
get carried away with strategies.

Young people need models, not critics.

Winning can breed envy and distrust in others, and overconfidence and a lack of appreciation in those who enjoy it.

You want the best player you can get
and then try to mold him
into the type of player that
will work into your
particular system.

The best five players very, very seldom
make up the best team.

When you are a coach,
your greatest ally is the bench.

A player who has given his best
has given everything,
but one who has given
less than his best,
regardless of how good
it looks on the scoreboard,
has given almost nothing.

A player should not just be willing
to sacrifice his own interest
for the good of the team,
he should be eager to do so.

My job as a coach
is to convince the players that
conflicts cannot get in the way
of what the team has to do.

To me, there's no such thing as an overachiever.
We're all underachievers to different degrees.

Honors are very fleeting, just as fame is;
I cherish friendship more.

Quiet confidence gets the best results.

If you do your best,
never lose your temper,
and never be out-fought
or out-hustled,
you have nothing
to worry about.

You can't put dignity and personality
into a person who doesn't have any.

There is no clock-watching
when the leader has respect.

Pride is a better motivator than fear.

115

A coach is someone who can give correction without causing resentment.

Leaders shouldn't do all the talking.

Fairness is giving all people
the treatment they earn and deserve.
It doesn't mean treating everyone alike.

The goal is to satisfy
not everyone else's expectations,
but your own.

If you lead a team as coach,
parent, or businessperson,
you must have enthusiasm
or you cannot be industrious.
With enthusiasm you stimulate
others to increasingly
higher levels of achievement.

I used to tell my players at the beginning
of the season that they were going to receive
criticisms, some deserved, some not,
as well as praise, but their strength
and character would depend on
how well they accept
that praise and criticism.

I've always cautioned my teams.
"Respect your opponents, but never fear them."

The man who is not afraid of failure
seldom has to face it.

The best thing you can do in public relations
is just to be a polite person that has
interest in other things as well as
your own profession.

Coaches aren't being honest with themselves
when they say they'd rather be the underdog
I'd much rather be the favorite.

I try to be very firm.
You may have to raise your voice a little
but yelling is a definite weakness.
I think it's like the use of profanity.
I think it's a weakness if you have to use it
to get your point across.

Musings

The worst thing about new books
is they keep us from reading the old ones.

Books are meant to be read.

There are many things that are essential
to arriving at true peace of mind,
and one of the most important is faith,
which cannot be acquired without prayer.

Winning has always been
the frosting that made the cake a little tastier.

The most important lesson
to teach a child is consideration for others.
You've learned so much along the way.

Anybody who does not put pressure
on himself is not worth much.
But if we permit outside pressure
to influence us very much,
we wouldn't be worth very much.

If I could choose the ideal player,
I'd choose someone who could play
defense, offense, was quick, unselfish,
team-oriented, and no problem
on or off the court and a good student.

One point at a time.

Oh Lord, make me beautiful within.

Success is peace of mind,
which is a direct result of self-satisfaction
in knowing you made the effort
to become the best of which you are capable.

A man there was they called him mad,
the more he gave, the more he had.

131

I've always felt that quickness
is the most important physical asset
an athlete can have.
Naturally, you want as much size
as you can get
to go with the quickness,
but if I had to sacrifice
one for the other,
it would be size every time.

Recorded history shows that
the underlying reason for the failure
of every civilization or cause has been
because of the breakdown from within
and I deeply believe that most potentially
great athletic teams that did not measure up
to what seemed possible and logical failed
because of friction from within.
Let us not be victimized
in such a manner.

I believe a sharp commanding
tone of voice
gets better results
when you're not there
working on things together.
It makes you snap,
be a little more with it.
When you're talking with
players privately,
I think a calm, pleasant,
almost comforting approach
is better except for rare individuals.

134

Regarding drills:
I don't want it become monotonous for them.
I want them to respond to each drill.
I've found that if you extend any one thing
very long, certain individuals with short
attention spans will become careless.

Since it has been established that
the learning processes are closely related
to physical, mental, and emotional fatigue,
it is not wise to continue past the point
where such a condition becomes apparent.
This is particularly true once the team
has attained good physical condition.
In your early season practices it may be
advisable to continue conditioning drills
a few minutes each day past the point
where they are tired but never
try to teach past that point.

Players now feel more things should be explained to them completely.... [T]hat's always been part of my teaching method, explaining the purpose of a thing to get the best result. But now some might even like to debate an issue with you. Discussion is all right, but I don't think it's right on the practice floor. I have my practices planned meticulously, and if I take time out for this, I won't have time for that. If they have complaints and want to talk to me afterwards, that's perfectly all right.

Get the players in the best of condition.
Teach them to execute the fundamentals quickly.
Drill them to play as a team.

You can't let praise or criticism get to you.
It's a weakness to get caught up in either one.
Some criticism will be honest, some won't.
You have to take both in the same light.

I consider cohesion to be extremely important.
I believe three things are vital for team success:
the ability to quickly and properly execute
the fundamentals, team play and team spirit,
and consideration for others. That's cohesion,
working together and being considerate of others.
A thorough proficiency in the fundamentals
enables each player to adjust quickly and
counteract whatever the other team might throw
at us. That way we can execute something
without thinking too long about how
we're going to do it.

The coach must never forget that he is a leader, not just a person with authority. The youngsters under his supervision must be able to receive proper guidance from him in all respects and not merely in regard to the proper playing of the game of basketball. The coach much be extremely careful in his judgment and consider all matters in the clear light of common sense. He must have a sense of discretion and tact comparable to that of Solomon. A sense of values in regard to men, games, techniques, and training is a must for him.

Why

Why
are there so many who want to
build up the weak by tearing down the strong?

Why
is it that many non-attainers
are very quick to explain and belittle
the attainers?

Why
are there so many who cannot
seem to realize that winners are
usually the ones who merely execute better,
at least on that particular occasion?

Why
is it so difficult to realize that
you cannot antagonize and influence
at the same time?

Why
is it that we are so slow to understand
that failing to prepare is preparing to fail?

144

Why
can't we realize that it only weakens
those we want to help when we do things
for them that they should do for themselves?

Why
is it so much easier to complain about
the thing we do not have, than to make
the most of and appreciate the
thing we do have?

Why
is it that it is so much easier to give others
blame than it is to give them credit?

Why
is it that many who are
quick to make
suggestions
find it difficult to make
decisions?

147

Why
don't we realize that others
are certain to listen to us
if we first listen to them?

Why
aren't we more interested
in finding the best way
rather than having our own way?

Why
is it much easier to be a critic
than a model?

Why
is it so hard to disagree
without being disagreeable?

Why
is it so difficult to realize,
at times,
that nothing we can do
will change the past,
and the only way
to affect the future
is by what we do now?

Why
is it that so often we permit
emotion rather than reason
to control our decisions?

Why
is it so difficult to develop
the feeling that those under our supervision
are working with us and not for us?

Why
can't we understand that all progress
comes through change even though
all change may not be progress?

Why
is it that we often forget
that big things are accomplished
only by the perfection of minor details?

152

Why
do we dread adversity so much,
when facing it is the only way
to become stronger?

Why
can't we motivate ourselves
when we know that results
come through motivation?

Why
is it that some seem ashamed
to let others know that they
pray or read the Bible?

Why
is it difficult to give thanks,
express thanks, or merely say,
"Thank you?"

154

Why
can't we have patience and expect
good things to take time?

Why
is it so easy to be quick to judge
when possessed of only a few facts?

Why
is it so easy to see
the faults of others
and so difficult to see
our own?

Ten Helpful Hints

One:
Be quick without hurrying.

Two:
Show me what you can do, don't tell me.

Three:
It is the little details that make things work.

Four:
The harder you work, the more luck you will have.

Five:
Respect every opponent, but fear none.

Six:
Hustle makes up for many a mistake.

Seven:
Valid self-analysis means improvement.

159

Eight:
Be more interested in character than in reputation.

Nine:
There is no substitute for hard work
and careful planning.

Ten:
Is it hard for you to keep quiet
when you don't have anything to say?

160

Wisdom From Coach's Dad

Advice

Be true to yourself.

Make each day your masterpiece.

Help others.

Drink deeply from good books.

Make friendship a fine art.

Build a shelter against a rainy day.

Joshua Wooden's Two Sets of Threes
Never lie, never cheat, never steal.
Don't whine, don't complain, don't make excuses.

The Adopted Creed

Four things a man must do
if he would make his life more true;
to live without confusion clearly;
to love his fellow man sincerely;
to act from honest motives purely;
to trust in God and Heaven securely.

Ten Things

I Learned From Coach

One:
Keep your cool. No matter what has happened,
"This too shall pass." You can surmount,
resolve or avoid many, if not most, obstacles
but you need to act with reason, not emotion.

Two:
When an error occurs, take action
as soon as possible. By doing so, oftentimes
it can be rectified. Humans make mistakes.

166

Three:
There is no substitute for hard work.

Four:
You can accomplish what you want,
even dream, if you are focused,
organized and have a realistic goal.
It is never too late to create
and accomplish goals.

Five:
Never stop learning.

Six:
Change is inevitable.
Always seek a better way, be ready to adapt.

Seven:
Family is first.

Eight:
Don't worry about the "other guy,"
the competition, the adversary.
Learn, follow and execute
the fundamentals of your endeavor.

Nine:
You cannot fool the person in the mirror.
It is your character that counts, not what
other people think of you. Keep your self-respect.
Be honest with yourself.

Ten:
The two most important words
in the English language
are "love" and "balance."

The John Wooden Pyramid of Success

SUCCESS

Peace of mind which is a direct result of self-satisfaction in knowing you did your best to become the best that you are capable of becoming . . .

John R. Wooden

John R. Wooden, Head Basketball Coach, Emeritus, UCLA

FAITH *(through prayer)*

PATIENCE *(good things take time)*

FIGHT *(determined effort)*

INTEGRITY *(purity of intention)*

COMPETITIVE GREATNESS
Be at your best when your best is needed. Enjoyment of a difficult challenge.

RESOURCEFULNESS *(proper judgment)*

RELIABILITY *(creates respect)*

POISE
Just being yourself. Being at ease at any situation. Never fighting yourself.

CONFIDENCE
Respect without fear. May come from being prepared and keeping all things in proper perspective.

ADAPTABILITY *(to any situation)*

HONESTY *(in thought and action)*

CONDITION
Mental - Moral - Physical Rest, exercise and diet must be considered. Moderation must be practiced. Dissipation must be eliminated.

SKILL
A knowledge of and the ability to properly and quickly execute the fundamentals. Be prepared and cover every little detail.

TEAM SPIRIT
A genuine consideration for others. An eagerness to sacrifice personal interests or glory for the welfare of all.

AMBITION *(for noble goals)*

SINCERITY *(keeps friends)*

SELF-CONTROL
Practice self-discipline and keep emotions under control. Good judgment and common sense are essential.

ALERTNESS
Be observing constantly. Stay open-minded. Be eager to learn and improve.

INITIATIVE
Cultivate the ability to make decisions and think alone. Do not be afraid of failure, but learn from it.

INTENTNESS
Set a realistic goal. Concentrate on its achievement by resisting all temptations and being determined and persistent.

INDUSTRIOUSNESS
There is no substitute for work. Worthwhile results come from hard work and careful planning.

FRIENDSHIP
Comes from mutual esteem, respect and devotion. Like marriage it must not be taken for granted but requires a joint effort.

LOYALTY
To yourself and to all those depending upon you. Keep your self-respect.

COOPERATION
With all levels of your co-workers. Listen if you want to be heard. Be interested in finding the best way, not in having your own way.

ENTHUSIASM
Brushes off upon those with whom you come in contact. You must truly enjoy what you are doing.

THE PYRAMID OF SUCCESS

If you enjoyed this book you may also enjoy *The John Wooden Pyramid of Success*.

Look for it in stores and online everywhere.

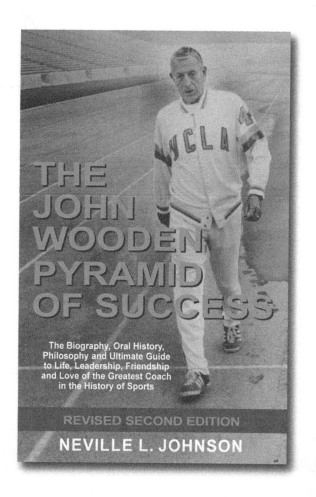

Find more cool books at CoolTitles.com